is for **Directions**

A Guide to Running

Confidence Building Courses for

Men of All Ages

Lesley Wilson

Mary Blair

and

Pat Armstrong

Russell House Publishing

First published in 2002 by:
Russell House Publishing Ltd.
4 St. George's House
Uplyme Road
Lyme Regis
Dorset DT7 3LS

Tel: 01297-443948
Fax: 01297-442722
e-mail: help@russellhouse.co.uk
www.russellhouse.co.uk

British Library Cataloguing-in-publication Data:
A catalogue record for this book is available from the British Library.

ISBN: 1-903855-18-7

Typeset by Jeremy Spencer, London. Cover photograph by Hemera.

Printed by Ashford Press, Southampton

About Russell House Publishing

RHP is a group of social work, probation, education and youth and community work practitioners and academics working in collaboration with a professional publishing team. Our aim is to work closely with the field to produce innovative and valuable materials to help managers, trainers, practitioners and students.

We are keen to receive feedback on publications and new ideas for future projects.

For details of our other publications please visit our website or ask us for a catalogue. Contact details are on this page.

Contents

Introduction

D is for Directions is a personal development manual for groupwork facilitators working with men. The exercises contained in this manual are designed to unlock the doorways to better self knowledge and understanding. They do this by enabling participants to establish a point of reference from where their journey of self discovery begins. They also allow participants to share experiences with others and offer a range of life skill tools which promote self acceptance and increase inner confidence.

We have called it D is for Directions for a reason. Our experience of working with men has taught us that men feel more comfortable working with realities rather than concepts. Confidence is a concept and means different things to different people. Directions are real. There are relevant questions to be asked about them and choices to be made. They are a great starting point to life adventures.

> *He's fine really, he only needs a bit of direction and the only one who can give it to him is, himself.*

Anyone who has felt a bit lost on life's journey knows that a little bit of help from the occasional passing stranger or signpost is greatly appreciated. This is one of the reasons we have put together this book.

D is for Directions includes exercises we have designed and developed through our experience of working with men in groups. We believe we have a formula that will enable you to put together your own training course with the reassurance that all materials have been tried and tested.

Lesley Wilson, Mary Blair, and Pat Armstrong have a broad base of experience from working in a wide variety of community projects. They now offer personal development, training and consultancy services through their Edinburgh based consultancy business, Inspire.

D is for Directions:
- Helps you plan and organise your own confidence building course.
- Gives you a choice of really useful exercises.
- Encourages you to feel confident as a facilitator.
- Identifies key readings which will develop your understanding of personal development for men.

How to Use this Manual

This manual has been designed as a 'pick up and use' tool. Depending on your needs, you can follow our approach to confidence building from start to finish, or you can dip in and pull out exercises that are appropriate to your group. Some exercises require handouts. These are set out on separate pages that can be easily photocopied and are marked with a ★ at the top of the page.

Running Confidence Building Courses for Men: Our Approach

Now, more than ever groups of men are meeting together to work on the issues that affect their lives. The time is right we feel for the companion edition to C is for Confidence (a guide to running confidence building courses for women), and thus, D is for Directions has evolved. The process is, a bit of self-exploration, a bit of pro-active investigation followed by strategies that can affect and maintain life changes. All this should be done using best practice group work. Our recent experience of working with men has shown that they are open to the process of change and ready to acknowledge the need for help to make those changes happen.

Group leaders have been using C is for Confidence for some time now. We have been told many times that it is a great pick up and go tool and is insightful in the process that it takes groups through. The process is a conscious engaging of internal and external factors to a depth (different for each individual), which results in a change in their perception of themselves. This process is not complicated, but it is extremely precarious. It is like making a good wine, all the ingredients must combine at the right time and in the right quantities.

Working with people must be the most frustrating and rewarding job in the world. You can achieve results far beyond your expectations, but you cannot control the process. Things will not go as expected.

The process is not easy – for tutors or participants. The tutor's task is to develop a programme in which participants challenge themselves, taking each step in personal development as steadily as is comfortable for them. Undoubtedly, with each new group of participants, tutors take on a huge responsibility. But, we are not responsible for participants' lives. Our responsibility is to show them a selection of tools for building confidence. It is then their responsibility to choose what they want, and put them into use. Some will reject it all, saying it's not for them. But they will leave with more than they came. Each experience, whether good or not so good, offers opportunities. Some will pick up everything they can carry, diving into self exploration with enthusiasm. They feel exhilarated, alive and eager to start afresh.

So how do we actually do this? We normally work with groups of eight to twelve men, running for two hours per week for ten weeks. We use a range of exercises and activities designed to be enjoyable and non-threatening which focus on individual experiences.

The first aim is to encourage sharing. Isolation of thought and experience is the most powerful barrier to change. In a ten week course, running for two hours per week, this period may last from two to five weeks.

After this the exercises are less emotional and less introspective. Participants begin to recognise the powerful tools they already have at their disposal. They begin to examine their lives, their roles in society and to question long-held perceptions. It is crucially important to give men space to flex their intellect. The men we have worked with are bright, clever, talented, creative and powerful, yet often have no concept of those aspects of themselves.

Next we look at strategies. Men support each other in their plans. They have made connections, friends and allies.

Ending a course is as important as the beginning. Men are more confident by the end. They feel more powerful, but are about to lose the support of weekly sessions with the group. They are often reluctant to let go, saying 'but what next?' However, by this time, they will have a bag of tools, some new friends, and several options to consider. Our whole philosophy is about moving on. To bring assistance to as many people as possible, we need participants to move on. And so, ending is turned into a celebration of what has been, and is yet to be accomplished.

An **A** to **Z** Guide to Running Confidence Building Courses

A is for Alien and Alliances

Working with men in groups is often seen as an **A**LIEN concept, both for the facilitator and the group members. The way that men experience socialisation teaches them that they must be self-sufficient and not needy. The truth is that these days, the role of men within our society has changed to such a degree that men are now experiencing isolation and marginalisation as never before. Working together through a group process is a fantastic learning experience, which lends itself particularly to the concept of personal development and life change.

Once taken through the initial stages, men will form new **A**LLIANCES, of a different value to those relationships they are traditionally associated with.

B is for Books and Building Trust

Resources relating to working with men are few and far between (which is why we're writing this one!). However we have included a few of our favourite **B**OOKS at the end of this manual.

BUILDING a trusting relationship with your group is key to the success of the course and you as facilitator must work hard at team building from session one.

C is for Childcare, Caffeine, Competition and Certificates

Crèche is hugely important as nowadays many men take full or partial responsibility for childcare and offering crèche or **C**HILDCARE expenses will encourage attendance.

CAFFEINE gives energy and if you provide freshly roasted coffee and tasty Assam tea, not only will your venue smell wonderful, but the group will feel that they are being valued too!

COMPETITION is something we are all familiar with. We are given messages throughout our lives that we must compete with each other, to be 'the best'. Reassure your group that this course focuses on personal development and that the only person you are competing with is yourself.

CERTIFICATES are important because some group members may have had a very negative past experience of education, perhaps gaining few or no qualifications. There is no formal qualification attached to confidence building, however, if you can design a certificate for your own course and present it to each member at the end, then again you are acknowledging the importance of the step that has been taken. The braver amongst you might even consider asking the group to design their own certificate as a closing exercise!

D is for Delivery and Diplomacy

The approach to **D**ELIVERY that you take as facilitator is crucial to the success of the course. We recommend that an informal approach works best. Start this approach by arranging the group sitting in comfy seats, in a circle, rather than in rows like a classroom.

DIPLOMACY is an essential skill required by all good facilitators. Group dynamics are well covered in other books. All we want to say is to be aware of the different opinions that will emerge within discussions and make sure you create a safe and non-threatening environment for all members to participate.

E is for Evaluation, Environment and Equality

It is difficult to measure the progress that groups make from the beginning to the end of a course like this one. **E**VALUATION is one way of finding out how the course is progressing. We have included various methods for participants to assess their progression throughout the book.

Make sure that the room that your group meets in is as aesthetically pleasing an **E**NVIRONMENT as possible, and warm. Cold rooms lead to cold groups.

To ensure **E**QUALITY, make sure the group members have an opportunity to have some control over their experience. Facilitators have a responsibility to let go sometimes and let the process happen.

F is for Friendly, Facilitator and Fear

FRIENDLY **F**ACILITATORS combat **F**EAR of participants, their behaviour sets the scene for the group. Need we say more?

G is for Ground Rules, Games and Goals

GROUND **R**ULES are an absolute essential for a group with participants who are taking part in probably one of the most difficult things they will ever have to do in their lives. It's better not to start the first session with ground rules. Wait until later in the session, once you have built a relationship with the group and they feel more comfortable. Make sure you include them as a closure – ground rules establish acceptable behaviour within the group and help set the tone for the remaining sessions.

GAMES are important components of any personal development course however many group members may have forgotten how to play! We've included some crackers in this manual.

Tell prospective group members that you will be running a session on **G**OALS and they'll be registering for your course in droves, particularly if they are football supporters!

H is for Honesty, Help and Humour

Making changes needs a lot of **H**ONESTY, firstly with yourself and then with others.

It is one of the key elements that enables us to get the **H**ELP we need. Remember, 'no man is an island' and it's OK to ask for help.

HUMOUR will flow naturally through your group if you have created the right atmosphere. This does vary, depending on the participants so use our jokes to get them started.

I is for Ideas, Inspiration and Imagination

This book is meant to give you a kick start, so when the **I**DEAS come which fit the needs of your group in particular, get out there and make them become a reality.

INSPIRATION can come from group members too. The old favourite 'aha' moment is always a pleasure to watch as well as experience.

Encourage people to use their **I**MAGINATION. Often it's been bashed out of us by the system. Use your open approach to allow your group to experience it once more.

J is for Judgement and Jokes

None of us is completely non-judgemental but it is something we should be aware of and discuss in the ground rules session. To grow as individuals we need to examine why we make the **J**UDGEMENTS we do, especially irrational ones. They may be holding us back.

JOKES are for everyone and against no-one.

K is for Kingpin and Knowledge

The trick of a good group is that the position of **K**INGPIN should move around and everyone should have a chance to experience it. Someone who wants to hold the position permanently should be reminded of the ground rules as set by the group themselves.

The **K**NOWLEDGE within your group will be vast. Tapping into this appropriately is a skill.

L is for Listening and Laughing

LISTENING to each other sharing thoughts and ideas can be the catalyst for real change. Groups do not do this naturally, they must be guided through the etiquette of listening while others are talking and not interrupting even when they have something really relevant to say.

LAUGHING is great. Laughing often expels nerves and 'up tightness'. Laughing energises and some say can heal.

M is for Men

MEN are individuals and a person-centred approach should always be taken.

N is for Noise and Nibbles

NOISE coming from your group is great. The buzz of the small groups means that they are communicating and you are half way there. Noise outside can't be helped sometimes but if at all possible, lose it.

Never forget the power of feeding people. Some select **N**IBBLES for coffee time can smooth out ruffles, which may have appeared during the first part of the session.

O is for Outings, Opinions and Openness

An **O**UTING with your group in the later stages of the course would be of great advantage. Choose something completely new for everyone. This could range from a visit to a local computer company, to a trip to the flicks. (The Full Monty was a memorable success!)

OPINIONS are most of what comes out of our mouths most of the time and that's fine, as long as they have some basis in reality. Opinions are good for starting off discussion and argument.

OPENNESS is to be encouraged and again it's up to the facilitator to set the standard.

P is for Power and Pressure

Be aware of **P**OWER struggles within groups. This can be part of the normal 'forming / storming' but a good facilitator can keep it under control.

Do not underestimate the effect that external **P**RESSURE can have on participants. Where possible, give them the space and opportunity to express these pressures and use the group to help work through strategies for coping.

Q is for Quality and Questions

QUALITY assurance should run through your course from top to bottom.

Create the atmosphere for asking **Q**UESTIONS. This is the way you and your participants will learn.

R is for Refereeing, Responsibility and Reality

Hopefully you won't need to do too much **R**EFEREEING. If people begin to get a bit heated, take at least one deep breath to give the rest of the group a chance to resolve things.

In the end, of course, you as the facilitator have some **R**ESPONSIBILITY to keep the peace in order to allow the group to progress.

Sometimes during the course people may become a bit removed from **R**EALITY. They may say why are we doing this? What has this got to do with anything? This is why you need to know why doing an exercise about your dad can lead to you getting the job or the place at college you have always wanted.

S is for Sabotage, Sabotage, Sabotage!!!

If you have a group member or maybe two who keep **S**ABOTAGING the sessions, you must act. The gigglers and the 'sniggerers' are really annoying but the truth is more likely to be that they feel scared and don't know how to express themselves. Sabotage is sometimes accompanied by phrases such as 'What's the point of this?', 'I just can't think of anything' or 'I don't want to do this'. Sabotage can occur for several reasons. It can be caused by genuine confusion on the part of the participant as to what he is supposed to be doing. In this case, a few minutes taken aside to explain, in a different way, the purpose of the exercise, may be all that is required. It can also be caused by participants feeling exposed, and outwith their comfort zone. Once again, empathy on the part of the facilitator is required. In the case of the gigglers, asking a direct question (would you like to share the joke with the rest of the group?) can draw their attention and you can then steer the group back to the task in hand.

T is for Timing, Tapes and Tact

Getting the **T**IMING right for the group can be the difference between continuing the group session or not. You know your client group better than us but these are a few things you need to take into account: bank holidays, school holidays, The World Cup, The Olympic Games, Wimbledon. No seriously though, think about work, school and meal timings and remember you are the one with the flexibility so make it work.

TAPES and other multi-media special effects can be used to jazz up a session. You can use tapes to relax to and to listen to music that inspires. Be creative and listen to what your group might want.

TACT is good but sometimes something difficult, disturbing or possibly provocative, just has to be said. A good facilitator will be able to find a diplomatic approach to difficult issues without causing hurt or offence to participants.

U is for Understanding and United

A level of **U**NDERSTANDING of participants' issues is essential for good facilitation. This can be gained from simply listening to their views with an open mind.

The best bit about learning and experiencing in a group together is when the group becomes **U**NITED. This is really what the experience is all about. In this form the individuals become stronger in themselves and change happens more easily.

V is for Venue and Versatile

Your **V**ENUE says everything about you, so make it good.

You have to be versatile if things are not progressing in the way you feel they should. That is when you sometimes have to throw the planned schedule away, be **V**ERSATILE, and pull another rabbit out of the hat.

W is for women

You should be aware of the influence that **W**OMEN may have in the lives of your participants. Whether from their upbringing by their mother or from their current partner, issues may arise that are not necessarily from the participants' own viewpoints.

X is for Xenophobia

Racial intolerance is sad and weak and just holds people back and definitely needs to be identified. **X** marks the spot.

Y is for You and Young People

YOU, as facilitator, can feel like you have a huge responsibility to keep the group progressing. However, the rewards of seeing individuals develop towards their full potential more than makes up for the stress involved!

This guide is for working with men of all ages. The exercises can be adapted to suit **Y**OUNG PEOPLE. Looking at the dreams we have as young people can be an important part of the process of fulfilling our dreams as adults.

Z is for Zany

Being **Z**ANY is always useful when things get a bit flat. This can range from the funny walk exercise to the Groucho Marks spectacles, which never fail to liven things up.

Step by Step Exercises

List of Exercises

Stage 1
Icebreakers for Every Mood, Opportunity or Occasion

Icebreakers are simple exercises, which take the pressure off being in a group for what may be the first time since school days. Their purpose is to encourage participants to get to know one another in a non-threatening, non-competitive way. Make them light and fun. Take time with icebreakers, especially over the feedback. They will set the tone for each session. Remember, it's the process that's important.

Paired introductions

Introduce yourself to your partner and find out who he is.

Feedback to the whole group with each pair introducing each other – 'Hi, I'd like to introduce my partner. This is Bob', and so on around the group.

Or try this

Find out who your partner is and another three things about him. Choose one of those things to tell the group when you introduce him.

Or this

Find out who your partner is and what makes him unique – (e.g. a hidden tattoo).

Or even this

Find out who your partner is and something a bit quirky about him – (e.g. he has never liked football).

Or you could try

Find out who your partner is and something that you each have in common (lack of direction is not allowed).

Or

Find out who your partner is and what he had for breakfast this morning.

Turn things around for...

Arrange the required number of chairs less one, in a circle. One group member volunteers to start the exercise off by standing in the middle of the circle whilst everyone else sits down. The person in the middle says 'Turn things around for...' (and completes the sentence) – e.g. 'everyone with blue eyes'. Anyone with blue eyes has to change seats and the person in the middle has to find a seat. Whoever is left standing then takes their turn to complete the sentence. This should be a fast moving exercise.

Call my bluff

Each group member is given a blank sheet of paper. They write their name in the middle of the sheet. In each of the four corners they write a statement. Three must be true and one must be false. In turn, they introduce themselves and read out their statements to the group.

The others must decide which is the false statement. This exercise is a great way of opening up the group and learning more about each other. After the whole group has completed the exercise, ask each group member in turn, if they would like their false statement to be true. Their answers might surprise you (and them!)

Ferrari, Fiesta or Fiat?

The facilitator must bring their artistic skills into play and draw each of the cars on the flipchart. (Don't worry if you're not artistic – this in itself is an icebreaker!)

Ask participants to consider which of these cars they feel themselves to be most like. Once they have had a chance to think, tell them to go and find others in the group who have chosen the same car as them. Tell them to talk about what it means to them to be like a Ferrari, a Fiesta or a Fiat. Share feedback with the whole group.

Or try this

When you ask participants to find others who are in their car grouping, tell them that they cannot speak but must communicate initially using the sound of their chosen cars engine!

Or even this

After participants have completed the first part of the exercise – 'Which car do you feel you are most like?' – ask them if they would prefer to be like something else.

Or else

You could replace the Ferrari, Fiesta or Fiat with other role models – e.g. characters from different soap operas or a variety of sportsmen.

Bridge building

Get a varied assortment of materials together, – e.g. an empty cereal packet, an old spool of cotton, pipe-cleaners, some string etc., and a toy car. Ask the group to build a bridge, which will hold the weight of the toy car, enabling it to be driven over, without the bridge collapsing. Leave the room and let the group get on with it. Give them 20 minutes to complete. This is a great team building exercise and should be introduced later on in the course when the group members know each other a little. The group themselves should be asked to judge how well they did.

Jokes

The worse the better!

Try:

- Where do astronauts park their spaceships? At a parking meteor!

- Knock knock: Who's there? Boo, Boo who? No need to cry, its just me!

- Why do authors look a bit strange? Because they have 'tales' coming out of their mouths!!

- Go round the group, one by one, challenging them to come up with something worse!

- A good one to get the group going when things are a bit flat.

Wasssssup?

The facilitator asks the group to shout 'Wassssup?' (as in the well known television advertisement for an American lager).

Each member of the group has to take a turn to tell the others something that has happened to them since the last session. All group members shout 'Wasssssup?' before the next person takes their turn.

This exercise is loud and funny and contemporary. It can also give group members who would like more opportunities to perform, to do so.

Ground Rules

Team tactics

At the beginning of any course it is important to spend time discussing how group members want their group to operate. This gives everyone a sense of ownership within the group, gives clarity about the purpose and process that the course will follow and is a fantastic fall back for facilitators in those nasty moments when it feels like the world is turning upside down!

Red card, yellow card

Give out one set of yellow cards and one set of red cards. Using the yellow cards first, ask each participant to jot down the things that they think make a group or a team, work well. (Encourage them to reflect on any previous experience they may have had.)

Then using the red cards, ask them to write down the things that destroy team work.

The cards are then read out and written on the flipchart by the facilitator. Through group discussion, ground rules are set, which can then be revisited during the course. Important – these are group ground rules and responsibility for them does not lie with the facilitator alone.

Or you could try

'Hopes and Fears' cards instead of 'red card, yellow card'.

Or else

Brainstorm 'Our Group values...' 'Our Group rejects...'

We would recommend copying ground rules for each participant, revisiting them in the following session, in case any changes have to be made and returning to them if things seem to be breaking down at any point in the course.

Stage 2
The Investigation Begins...

Confidence building is an experiential process. Men come to the course wanting to increase their confidence, wanting to make changes in their lives. It is important that there is a benchmark from which any progress can be measured. The following exercises will help the process unravel.

What league am I in?

This exercise helps group members to identify where they are right now in their lives. Facilitators should photocopy the sheet opposite for each member of the group. Working individually, the task is to mark which league you place yourself in right now and to fill in the corresponding section 'What does this mean to me?'.

There is no group discussion at this stage, though handouts should be retained by participants and reviewed at the end of the course. In the final review, the whole group discussion should focus on where participants are now and how important this sort of exercise is.

Photocopy the page opposite to use with your group. →

What league am I in?

Think about where you are in your life **right now**! Go with your gut instinct and place yourself in the middle column. Do it quickly and you will find that you automatically feel more comfortable writing in whichever box seems right. Jot down your ideas about what being in that league means to you. Now look at the options you didn't fill in and decide which one you want to be in. Jot down any ideas about what you need to do to get there.

What does this mean to me?	Premier League	What do I need to do to get here?
What does this mean to me?	First Division	What do I need to do to get here?
What does this mean to me?	Second Division	What do I need to do to get here?
What does this mean to me?	Pub Team	What do I need to do to get here?

What is confidence?

If you ask people 'What is confidence?' you will get a variety of responses. Confidence means different things to different people. It is important to acknowledge this fact to your group and to show them that confidence is about perception. These exercises will help to start the process of demystifying what confidence is. The group will start to examine confidence objectively, perhaps for the first time.

Use the handouts 'What is confidence?' and 'What does confidence mean to me?'

In pairs, get group members to make a list of their ideas about what confidence is. For example, singing at a karaoke party, buying underwear for your partner, admitting that you watch Coronation Street! You get the picture.

After ten minutes or so, get the whole group to discuss the ideas that they have come up with. You (and they) will be amazed with the assortment of different ideas that are in the group.

Then, again in pairs (but different ones this time), get the group to come up with a definition of what confidence actually means for them. You can get pairs to join up together and share their thoughts, working in this way until you are back as a whole group again. You may find that there are several definitions of what confidence means, and that's OK.

Photocopy the page opposite to use with your group. ➜

What is confidence?

Working in pairs, take a few moments to jot down your ideas.

Confidence is:

1.   Singing at a karaoke party

2.   Refusing that last pint!

3.   Crying at a soppy movie

4.

5.

6.

7.

8.

9.

10.

What does confidence mean to me?

Work in small groups to get a definition of confidence.

Who am I?

As we've already said, the initial stages of confidence building require participants to acknowledge where they are in their lives at this moment in time. They also need to explore who they are and recognise their own uniqueness, characteristics and personality traits.

Ask participants to look at the following statements and tick those which apply to them and fill out the blank statements at the bottom of the page. Work individually on this handout. Then in pairs discuss what these statements mean. Come back together as a whole group and discuss.

Photocopy the page opposite to use with your group. →

Who am I?

I am a man

I am a boy

I am a son

I am a father

I am a husband/partner

I am a teacher

I am a brother

I am a breadwinner

I am a worker

I am a thinker

I am a ....

The most confident man (and me)

Encourage group members to work individually on the following exercise:

Get them to fill in a photocopy of the Macho Man outline opposite, showing all the elements that they believe make him confident.

Get each participant to present their description to the full group and discuss.

Now get each participant to fill in a new outline for himself, showing which elements they believe they need to obtain in order to be more confident.

Ask participants to think about how they could encompass these elements into their life over the next week and feedback at the next session.

Photocopy the page opposite to use with your group. ➜

Meditation for the mind

The irony of your present eating habits is that while you fear missing a meal, you aren't fully aware of the meals you do eat.

Dan Millman, *Way of the Peaceful Warrior*, p118.

Do you sometimes think of dinner while you are still eating lunch? Lots of us do. It's one of the curses of life in the modern western world. We have so many things to stimulate our senses that we frequently block them all off as we speculate about the future. The next job, next holiday, next house, next thing to be done, even the next relationship! Our minds can sometimes go into overdrive.

The effect that this can have on our confidence and our reality can be devastating. We begin to lose track of who we are and start to value and measure ourselves by what we have or don't have.

Meditation gives us the opportunity to find our true self and is an activity that is no longer confined to the realms of 'daft stuff!'. Nowadays many famous sportsmen and successful businessmen acknowledge the usefulness of meditation.

A successful meditation will help you clear a space in your mind. This space may feel calm, peaceful, clear or restful. These are all positive states to be in. These feelings help us to reflect and plan effortlessly!

Introducing meditation to the group may feel a little scary, but the results can be mind-blowing! Set it as a confidence building challenge.

You need to find a quiet space and a time when you will not be interrupted. Tell participants to get comfy, but not to lie down. Meditation is not about falling asleep. Agree in advance the length of time you will spend on this activity. (Five minutes is a good start.)

Method One
Breath in and breath out.

Be aware of your breathing.

Breath in and count	One	on the out breath
	Two	
	Three	
	Four	
	Five	

Repeat from One

Read these instructions to the group five times as they practice. Then leave them for five minutes to continue on their own.

Method Two

Begin as above focusing on breathing instead of counting. Choose a word that inspires you. (You could try 'flip-charting' examples of inspiring words from the group before you start.) Each group member can have their own word and they don't have to share this with anyone. Each individual focuses on their word, saying it silently on each out breath.

Method Three

Begin as method one above focusing on breathing instead of counting. Each group member chooses an object they are familiar with. Tell them to picture the object in their minds eye. Instruct them to focus on the object, looking at it in more and more detail for five minutes.

Once you have introduced meditation to your group you might find that it becomes a regular exercise at the beginning or the end of each session.

Stage 3
Fact Finding and Setting the Scene

It is very important to be able to measure progress, not just for the group as a whole, but for the individuals within it and for you the facilitator. This can be achieved by using very simple, yet challenging 'scene setting' and 'fact finding' exercises, as detailed in this stage.

What's in a name?

Work individually, and then in pairs.

What is your full name?

How was it chosen?

What does it mean?

Do you like it?

What does it say about you?

What goes along with having this name?

What is positive about having this name?

What is negative about having this name?

If you could change your name, what would you change it to and why?

Whole group feedback and discussion.

Success is...

This exercise is designed to find out what being successful means to you. Participants are asked at the end of a session to bring back five things next week that for them as individuals are cause to say 'this is a success'.

It could be:
- a ticket from a football game
- first wage packet
- photo of their child

Participants take it in turn to talk about the things they have brought. They do this by completing the following sentence:

Success is.. because...

....

The other members listen until the participant has finished and are then allowed to ask questions.

Making movies!

This is about self-exploration and taking feedback and should be used in a group that feels as safe as possible.

The facilitator asks each group member to imagine that a movie is going to be made about them.

Each individual must answer the following questions:

1.   Who do you think will play the leading role and say why?

2.   Who do you think your friends would choose to play the lead and say why?

3.   Write down who you think should be playing each of your fellow participants in their movie and say why?

When everyone is finished, participants take it in turn to share their answers to one and two with the rest of the group. Only then do the others feedback their answers for question three. Keep it light and remind everyone it's just a bit of fun.

The facilitator then uses the following questions to reflect on:

How much do you play the role that you think others want you to play?

Would you like to change your role?

What changes would you make right now if you could?

How does it feel to be more true to you?

Sabotage

We all do it. We pretend we don't know why. But we do know. This is your chance to come clean and acknowledge those areas of your life that could do with a bit of re-focusing. Get together with a supportive group member and help each other to work on your own lists of the things you do to sabotage your life.

Example worksheet

S   Sloping off

A   Acting up

B   Backing away

O   Overbearing

T   Turning

A   Attacking

G   Going AWOL

E   Effing and blinding!

(or you could make up your own acronym)

Photocopy the page overleaf to use with your group. →

Things I do to sabotage my life

S

A

B

O

T

A

G

E

!

!

!

What people say (1)

Write the following statements on cards and hand out to group.

Take it in turns to discuss what the saying means and then decide if you agree or not?

Don't rock the boat

Grow up

Act like a man

Be your own man

Stick up for yourself

It's all good

The die is cast

You've made your bed so lie in it

Take it on the chin

Stop kidding yourself

What people say (2)

Write the following statements on cards and hand out to group.

Choose the statement which you most identify with and keep it in your mind until next time.

I am a genius now

I have the right to be successful

I can define my own success

Anything is possible

Reach for the stars

I can do anything I want to do

Be bold

He who dares wins

I can handle anything

I have everything I need

I am good enough right now

I am powerful

The usual suspects

Dads and sons: Rewriting the script

This exercise is about your history, genetic and social. There are things going on in your mind right now which you are not aware of. Thoughts and memories can, and do, affect our lives even when we don't know that they are there. Try this exercise and see what happens when you don't try to remember.

Let's start it off by diving into the unconscious mind.

We need paper and paints and a place where we can make some mess.

The task:

Your task is to mix a colour which represents your dad or the person you see as your chief male role model. Have some fun experimenting.

Then mix a colour for yourself.

Feedback to whole group.

This is the colour I have mixed for my dad and this is why................

This is the colour I have mixed for myself and this is why................

Questions:

Are you like your dad/role model?

In what ways?

Role models (1) and (2)

First ask the group to work on the following exercises individually.

Then get them to discuss what they have written in pairs.

Next feedback to the whole group, flipchart the answers and work with the group to identify common characteristics from the chosen role models.

Photocopy the following two pages to use with your group. →

Role models (1): Who are yours?

Who are the three men you most look up to?

1.

2.

3.

Why do you look up to these men?

1.

2.

3.

How have your role models affected your life?

1.

2.

3.

Role models (2): Who are yours?

Who are the three people you most look up to?

1.

2.

3.

Why do you look up to these people?

1.

2.

3.

How have your role models affected your life?

1.

2.

3.

Self esteem visualisation

Get your participants comfortable and relaxed and slowly read the visualisation. This is for you and you alone, you will not be sharing it with anyone so use your imagination and begin to experiment with a few new ideas.

Think about the last time you felt really good about yourself. A time when you were sure about what you wanted and where you wanted to go. Life was straightforward and easy. Concentrate on a particular event or day.
If you can't remember just make it up.

You must fill in all the details now. What do you see, what are the colours, are they clear and sharp?

....

Now, what do you hear, tune in to what's in the background, listen

....

Now what do you feel, mmhhhh, just feel it

Maybe you can taste something or smell something, sense it, enjoy it

....

Take your time to build the picture and then come back

Questions

How did it feel?

If you managed to do this exercise you have just been in touch with your confident self. You see he is in there all the time it's just that sometimes we can lose track of him.

Stage 4
The Breakthrough:
Change is Inevitable

The following exercises aim to demystify and take the fear out of change. They give the participants a chance to think about the implications of change and to realise that if nothing changes, *nothing changes*. One of the most important things to remember is, whether we are afraid or not, change will happen. In fact, change is probably one of the most constant aspects of our lives. It is how we deal with it that makes the difference.

Take a chance

This exercise is in the form of a game. Use a pack of playing cards. Each card will have a corresponding challenge. This exercise could be used to start or finish a session. The game we play is just like snap. We deal all the cards out and then play. When two cards the same appear then the person who calls out **challenge** has won. They look up the challenge referring to the card they have matched to find out what it is. If they like it they can keep it, if not they give it to the person who dealt the card. Once you have a challenge you leave the game and the remaining cards are dealt out to the others. The challenges could be written on a flipchart.

Example challenges:

- **Ace**   Go to your local leisure centre and do an activity you have never done before.
- **One**   Go into a shop you have never been in before.
- **Two**   Go to the library and get a book on something you don't know anything about.
- **Three**   For a whole day you must not sit in your usual seat.
- **Four**   For a whole week you must try something different for breakfast.
- **Five**   Go to your wardrobe and get rid of at least one thing you have not worn for a year.
- **Six**   Buy yourself an ice cream and eat it in public.
- **Seven**   Watch a sport on TV that you have never watched before.
- **Eight**   Try a different route to a usual destination.
- **Nine**   Make small talk with a stranger.
- **Ten**   Use a different type of transport.
- **Jack**   Buy something from a second-hand shop.
- **Queen**   Listen to a type of music you have never tried before.
- **King**   Meditate for five minutes every day.

Take a note of each participants challenge, and ask them to report back the following week on how it felt. The object of the exercise is to get participants used to the feeling of doing something different. It also introduces them to the idea that once they have actually completed the challenge, it doesn't feel so threatening anymore.

Mr Angry

The more we find out about ourselves the more we realise how much we don't know.

- What is anger?
- Where does it come from?
- Why do we need it?

Anger is just like any other emotion. In small doses it's just part of life but too much can stunt our growth. We don't really get much opportunity to explore our feelings of anger and this exercise can allow participants to do this in a safe way. Start off by having a brainstorm of things that make you angry.

Watch out because this can get your group really animated and you will need to acknowledge all the anger and then bring back calm.

Now tell your group that you are about to begin an exploration of the phenomenon of anger. You begin by identifying 10 people you have seen being angry about something. It does not matter if they were angry at you or at something else. Then go back and write down why you think they got angry. Then in pairs answer the questions.

Photocopy the page overleaf to use with your group. ➔

Angry!

Think of ten examples of people you have experienced getting angry

People   **Reasons for being angry**

1.

2.

3.

4.

5.

6.

7.

8.

9.

10.

Now go back and write down why you think they got angry.

In pairs answer the following questions. Don't rush, and ask one question at a time.

Questions:

Did getting angry get help?

Does getting angry act as time out from addressing the stuff I need to work on?

Does getting angry make you feel better?

Does getting angry ever work?

Back to the future

In order to move forwards, it is sometimes necessary to look back. This exercise gives participants an opportunity to look back at significant events in their lives and to reflect on how these events may have influenced them now and in the future.

Ask each member of the group to draw a route map using the following road signs as turning points in their lives. Ask them to explain at each road sign what it meant to them:

- roundabout
- T junction
- no entry
- stop sign
- 30 mile an hour limit
- national speed limit applies
- no parking
- no overtaking
- one way
- single lane traffic
- motorway ahead

Feedback to the group. This exercise will help participants to see which routes came to a stop and why and which routes were smoother.

Messages from the past and messages for now

In the process of building confidence, men are often given unhelpful messages. The next exercise allows participants to explore the negative messages which others have given them. On completion, the group should discuss the underlying message in what others have said to them. There should then be a symbolic 'scoring out' of the old messages before participants develop new, positive messages for themselves.

Photocopy the following four pages to use with your group. ➔

Messages from the past

Write a list of messages you have received about how to be you.

What my mum said

What my dad said

What the family said

What my teachers said

What my friends said

What work said

Messages for now

Write a list of things that you would like to tell them about you now!

Messages for my mum

Messages for my dad

Messages for the family

Messages for my teachers

Messages for my friends

Messages about work

Exercise for change (1)

Think about times in your life when change has occurred. Choose one change which was a good experience and one which was not so good.

My good experience was:

Were you responsible for this change?

How did you incorporate this change into your life?

What did you learn about yourself because of this change?

Are you glad that the change happened?

Could you have done anything to prevent the change?

Would you change anything if you could?

Is there any unfinished business that you need to deal with concerning this change?

Can you do anything about this now?

If you were advising a dear friend, what would you say about the way they dealt with this change?

Exercise for change (2)

My not so good experience of change was:

Were you responsible for this change?

How did you incorporate this change into your life?

What did you learn about yourself because of this change?

Are you glad that the change happened?

Could you have done anything to prevent the change?

Would you change anything if you could?

Is there any unfinished business that you need to deal with concerning this change?

Can you do anything about this now?

If you were advising a dear friend, what would you say about the way they dealt with this change?

Goals, goals, goals!!

Get participants to identify three goals that they want to achieve in their lifetime. Now ask them to think of something that they could do:

a) within the next week

   then

b) within the next month

   then

c) by the end of the year

   in order to make their goals come true.

This allows the group to understand that goals should be broken down into small manageable chunks.

Mind maps

Ask group members to draw a vehicle representing themselves. Any form of vehicle can be chosen (from a Porsche, to a mini or even a bus or a space ship!). Participants must now draw the different roads that their vehicle is going to travel along, then feedback to the whole group, answering the following questions, adding any detail:

1. What are the roads like that you are travelling on? e.g. hilly, straight, any obstacles.

2. What destination are you heading for?

3. What's the best way to get there?

4. Why did you choose this type of vehicle?

SMART

SMART goals must be:

Specific
Measurable
Achievable
Realistic
Time-limited

A well tried and tested exercise but your group may not have tried it before. Write the following on a flipchart. Ask individuals to choose a goal and detail as shown in the example below:

S	specific – getting a job
M	how is it measured – by being in employment
A	how will I achieve it – by sending my CV to at least 20 employers by the end of the month
R	being realistic – making realistic choices based on qualifications and experience
T	time to aim for – by the end of the year

The power of language

What if you could do anything or go anywhere – how would that change your life and the way you feel about yourself? In pairs discuss and then feedback to the whole group.

Well here's some good news, you can. The things that you tell yourself tend to come true. When you think 'I don't think I'll get the job'. The response is usually 'I didn't get that job'.

As we have mentioned before sometimes people get into such a stuck place that they can't imagine themselves anywhere else. This is why it is important to give them a task which seems to be one step removed from themselves, e.g. What if you had a friend who...

This is a powerful activity when we engage our imaginations to work on a process like this one. In order to do this exercise we need to be open to new ideas. If we can imagine good feelings, then we must know what they feel like. If we imagine powerful feelings then we feel powerful feelings. This type of exercise allows us to get in touch with inner experiences, like the confidence which we may not have felt for a while. It allows us to practice putting on the good feelings that are part and parcel of our growth.

Magical dream

Close your eyes and dream. Imagine someone you know, someone you like. Now, you are going to be given some magical powers. You are now a powerful wizard and you can give this person anything they want. Take some time to think about what you think they would like in their lives. You can't ask them so just let your imagination go wild. Remember there are no right or wrong answers:

- What are the things you think are important for this person?
- What would make them feel really good?
- What are the things that would make them happy?
- Where did you make all this happen?

Go forward in time now and see how this has all worked out.

See how happy this person is.

What is this person saying about their life?

Feeling pride

Feeling pride is one of the top ten good feelings and we need more practice. We can feel pride for our country, our football team, our children, our friends and so on, but often we have difficulty in feeling pride in the things that we do or play a part in ourselves. Low self-esteem thrives on isolation and cutting ourselves off from the things that make us feel good takes us to a lonely place. This is why we need to practice engaging with those good feelings and pride is a excellent place to begin. These three exercises should be done in the following order.

- Ten things other people have done that make me proud.
- Ten things in my life that make me feel proud.
- Ten things I have done that make me proud.

First thinking about the things and people 'out there' that make us proud. This is always the easiest way to start. Make sure that there is a break of at least one day, before taking on the next exercise. In this exercise we have to think of the things in our lives that make us proud. This is more personal than the first one. We need to begin to acknowledge that we have things in our lives of which we are proud.

Step three is powerful. It means acknowledging that we have done things we are proud of.

The things which are cited do not have to be big things, and this exercise does not have to be shared unless participants want to. The most important part of this exercise is that each time we think of a response we evoke the feeling of pride and it feels good.

Photocopy the following three pages to use with your group. →

Ten things other people have done that make me proud

1.

2.

3.

4.

5.

6.

7.

8.

9.

10.

Ten things in my life that make me feel proud

1.

2.

3.

4.

5.

6.

7.

8.

9.

10.

Ten things I have done that make me proud

1.

2.

3.

4.

5.

6.

7.

8.

9.

10.

Ten things I want to do before I die

We all have hopes and dreams and inner desires, but often everyday life gets in the way and we never quite make it happen. If you knew a child who had a dream, a dream that made them pink with excitement, would you encourage them in their dreams or not? What if you had a second chance to go for the things you wanted to go for? Well you have and it all starts here!

Go for it!

Photocopy the page opposite to use with your group. ➜

Make a list of ten things you want to do before you die. Now!

1.

2.

3.

4.

5.

6.

7.

8.

9.

10.

A slogan for the group

In small groups, work on the questions below to help you create a slogan for your group:

1. What is important to the people in this group?

2. What do you want to say about yourselves?

3. What do you want others to know about you?

4. What is the message you get from the answers above?

5. Can you turn it into something really catchy?

Our slogan is ....

....

Stage 6
Full Time: Reviewing and Ending

The following exercies allow you to finish on a high. Rounds are good for starting, finishing and ending. Try the other exercises to give the group the chance to review where they are at and to acknowledge the 'distance travelled' along the route to increased self confidence.

Rounds for all occasions

Take it in turns to go around the group, each member ending the statement:

Something that **surprised** me about today
was...

Something that **pleased** me about today
was...

Something that **confused** me about today
was...

Something that **delighted** me about today
was...

Something that **niggled** me about today
was...

Something that **tickled** me about today
was...

Something that **challenged** me about today
was...

Something that **bugged** me about today
was...

Something that **excited** me about today
was...

Slap on the back!

Everyone in the group gets a pile of stickers on which they must write a complimentary statement about everyone else in the group. These are then stuck on the backs on the appropriate group members. This is done simultaneously, so people are milling around slapping each other on the back. When everyone is done, you take it in turns for a partner to peel off the stickers and read them out loud to the rest of the group.

Confessions of the man in the street

Answer the following question in pairs.

Why I really, really haven't been behaving confidently!

Feedback to the whole group. This is a simple yet powerful review process.

Leaving on a high

Create an elevated spot in the room and invite participants one by one to take their place on high to address the group. They are received with tumultuous applause.

Symbolic gift

Use an object as a symbol – e.g. a paperweight, a trophy. Each participant gives another the gift saying why they want to give the other a gift. e.g: 'I would like to give you this gift because you always listen to what I have to say'. The object is passed around until everyone has received and given the gift.

Letting go and moving on

Read this short story and, as you read it, think about how Peter could take responsibility for his own life and not rely on others to make him happy.

Peter had spent quite a few years in Never Never Land now. Laughs all round, every day filled with games and carrying on. What could be more perfect? Then things began to change. Captain Hook, his great rival, had got a job in the Isle of Dogs looking after the canaries. Now there was no-one to fight with anymore. The lost boys had saved up enough money to go off on a round the world trip and would be away for the next six months. Peter had felt that it was a bit too much of a commitment, £50 quid a month for a year, and had preferred to spend his money as and when he pleased.

The prospect of spending the whole summer in Never Never Land with only Tinkerbell to keep him company was not inspiring. She only flew around having fun and never sat still. What would he do for stories now? He'd never realised what it felt like to be bored before. Why was no-one around to keep him amused?

Peter is feeling a bit stuck.

What can he do?

Who can he go to for help and advice?

Who is going to read to him now?

Ask the group to discuss the above questions and come up with some useful suggestions for Peter to improve his situation.

CERTIFICATE

OF CONFIDENCE

You have worked hard on your plan for change!

Well Done

Keep going you are doing really well!

Signed ....

Date ....

Appreciation Sheet

1. What changes, if any, have you become aware of in yourself or in your behaviour since you began your confidence building course?

2. In which areas of your life do you feel most confident now?

3. In which situations do you need more practice in being confident?

4. What are the three most important things that you have learned about yourself during this course?

Evaluation Sheet

What did you like most about the course?

What did you like least about the course?

What is the most important thing that you learned during the course?

What would you say to other people about the course?

Would you say that your confidence has increased during the course?

Would you make any changes to the course?

Further Reading

Buzan, T. with Buzan, B. *Mind-mapping*. BBC Books.

Edwards, G. *Living Magically*. Piatkus Books.

Harris, T. A. *I'm Okay, You're Okay*. Pan Books.

Harris, T. A. *Staying Okay*. Pan Books.

Jeffers, S. *Feel The Fear and do it Anyway*. Arrow Books.

Malz, M. *Psycho Cybernetics*. Wiltshire Book Co.

McGiverney, V. *Excluded Men: Men Who Are Missing From Education and Training*. NIACE.

Millman, D. *Way of the Peaceful Warrior*. H. J. Kramer.